Unbecoming Lost:

A meditative collection of self-study poems

Shaneeka "SHALOM" Goins

Made with ❤ on the BookLeaf Publishing Platform
www.bookleafpub.in
www.bookleafpub.com

Dedication

This book is dedicated to Gracie- Mama's Miracle.

Let this be a lesson that you can do anything you set
your mind to.
Thank you for the motivation to write on the days when
I wasn't "feeling it".
Thank you for pushing me to take this book from a
mental construct to a physical reality.

Mommy loves you.

Preface

Shaneeka SHALOM: I am I.

Let me begin with a personal creed:

I am a motivated, disciplined, educated, and productive member of my community.

I accept leadership opportunities in which my characteristics of creativity, intelligence, innovation, resilience, and well-being are utilized, respected, and appreciated.

I facilitate learning through mindful, self-affirming behaviors, in collaboration with remaining authentic through presentation of skill-development, while remaining conscious of the best outcomes and opportunities for individuals, society, and Earth.

I will move forward with courage, sincerity, balance, open-mindedness, cultural competence, and kindness to aid in manifesting a life that is stable, sustainable, connected, and diverse,

I am a lifelong yogi and I greatly appreciate the Yamas and Niyamas identified in the 8 Limbs of Yoga. Self-study translates to Svādhyāya - which is identified as a Niyamas (or "observances"). It seems only fitting that to have a meditative collection of self-study, it shall pay homage to the foundation for mind-expansion and begin with a true meditation:

Come to a seated position. Adjust as necessary, and
begin to notice your breath.
(PAUSE & breathe 5 seconds)
Breathe out.
Exhale.

As you continue to take intentional breaths, become
aware of the power within you. Each breath in welcomes
a fresh supply of the abundant energy available to
sustain you. Each exhale has the ability to let go and
release the moments of the days, the weeks, the months,
and years of built up moments and thoughts that no
longer serve you.

(PAUSE & breathe 5 seconds)

Your experiences belong to you. As you grow and
change, so does the message and lesson of the
experience. With the constant flow and exchange of
energy through your breaths and interactions, it is
available for you to take what you need in each moment,
while letting go of what you do not. The evolution of
your being is shaped by the intentionality of your intake
and release.

(PAUSE and breathe 5 seconds)

Take in the love you feel from the sun's warm embrace.
Release the tension in your body from a tough
conversation. Take in the beauty of the flowers blooming
as spring announces its arrival. Release the pieces of
your life story that do not radiate connectedness with
your true essence. You have the power. You are
empowered.
You are strong and being strengthened. Within you, you
have the answers and the key to everything you seek.
You are healing and you are whole. You are Universally
connected. And we are one.

(PAUSE and breathe 5 seconds)

Begin to bring your awareness back to your body.
Wiggle your toes and fingers. Flutter your eyes open as
you become aware of your surroundings.

Take what you have gained and leave what does not
serve you.

Namaste

Gratitude extended towards you for taking that first
meditative journey, with the understanding that there

are to be many more journeys throughout this collection of poems. Each poem will be focused on a feature- whether that be a perspective, a characteristic, a moral, an ethic, or a personal value. Let's begin!

Acknowledgements

I want to acknowledge my whole slew of instructors that I have been honored to meet throughout my academic and yogic career.

I also want to acknowledge my brother and sister, who helped me choose the perfect wording for my subtitle through preface, looked over multiple candidates for my cover photo, and reviewed countless revisions of poems throughout this writing and editing process. I love you so both so much!

1. Unbecoming Lost

Let me take you on a meditative journey of a girl
becoming found.

Imagine: Presenting as a sea of elegance, eloquence,
exquisiteness and poise.
Gliding hastily-yet effortlessly- amidst the chaos and the
noise.
Ambitious, Accomplished, Creative, Courageous and
Kind;
These words fueled your ego- but what about your
mind?

Pondering the duality of Bodies being Self-propagating
stations for spirits and souls....
Reduced to acronyms to equate significance in a world
that's grown so cold.
Perspectives.

Check in: Are you seeing it too?
Tell me, are you aware?
Is this self-actualization or the man upstairs?

Reincarnation, is that slavery?
Existentialism. Nihilism. Optimism.

This cycle repeats- mundanity.

Recognizing truths like choosing to live gives way to
both despair and delight.
Forged by fire, but hey at least you shine bright.
Somber moments and sweet memories,
intricately crashing together create the inner- me.

2. Melanin, Curls, and Beauty

Maybe I didn't
Even spell this word right.
Let me try again— BLACK.
Ancestry matters,
Nigga Neeka.
Induced you've been; hello
Nigger. -America

&

Can I touch it?
Usually I'd say yes, but
Really I have a new boundary.
Let me answer you
Softly, no.

&

Bouncy
Exotic or native?
Authentic
Ungrateful would be the perception because "luck"
explains
Tendrils that make you so
You-tastic! (*insert "smile")

3

3. Injected Individuation

It starts within and flows about.

It comes in waves while you go without.

Learnings of somatic memories,

understandings of chakra energies.

FREQUENCIES GUIDE THE ENTIRETY OF BEING.

4. Core Values

integrity,
authenticity,
courage,
compassion,

empathy,
innovation,
respect,
these never go out of fashion.

creativity,
kindness,
diversity,
and
cultural-competence.

learning,
accountability,
patience,
and balance.

peace,
genuineness,
open-mindedness,

resilience,
and
earth-consciousness.

sustainability,
passion,
skill-development,
self-care,

sincerity,
well-being,
mindfulness,
gratitude,
support,
community--
idenitification is a step in becoming self-aware.

5. Resilient

Relentless self-reliance- or did I mean resilience?
Courage in the face of adversity.
The parts that shape the wholeness in me.
Intergenerational trauma synonymous with generational curses.
Pain and sorrow in the bones of the ones who go before us.
Learnings that admirable qualities are trauma responses.
Challenging to accept, not downplaying- it's daunting.
Quick-witted, self-sufficient, and admittedly overzealous.
Discerning moments.
Envy or jealous?
Keys to unlock the psyche.
Knowledge of books and the streets.
Examine Your History.
Communication gateways into a world unknown.
Poetry, purpose, perception and prose.

6. WEllness

I'm going to experiment with a little haiku,
syllables in 5-7-5, a guide for you:

ikigai, future
learn, instructor, guru, sage
experiential

7. 7102

Zig zags, spiraling, falling down.
Where's left to go when you've hit the ground?
"Only up" is what they say;
every night I will continue to pray.
"Trust in Him with all your might. You've found Him-
He's brought the light".
Nights so cold and days so dark -- yes, it is a broken
heart.
2 cents left in my savings and no hope left in my soul;
"Keep going! Keep pushing!";
Okay, but I have nowhere left to go.
The light that used to burn so brightly is now nothing
more than dull.
There is solence in these bodies that at least share in my
home.

8. Wraparound Life

Wellness definition and application:
The ability to stay within your flow
-your personal life current-
without stagnation.
In my professional career,
I used to be known for facilitation.

Here's my takeaway I want to share
about the importance of approaches that show you care:

Bring people together.
Lead them in the process of seeing each other differently
and in a new light-
notice deeper connections,
acknowledge the importance of interdependence
and the spirit of counsel and might.
Strive towards cohesive collaboration.
Empathetic input breeds adoration.

Emotional and spiritual literacy
engulfs embarking in intimacy.

9. The Mother Wound

Here's a poem I wrote when I was a teenager.

Mom
I am now the glue that holds everything together.
Young in age yet wise at heart.
Putting others needs before my own.
I give and give, yet receive nothing in return.
I strive to do my best at every task thrown my way,
hoping and praying for better with the new day.
It seems nothing changes and I am always blue, the only
hope I have is to think of you.
I remember the good times and some of the bad,
they make me so happy and yet so sad.
I miss you so dearly words can't begin to explain- My
pain runs deep and through all of my veins.
Accomplishments you wanted I'm trying to embrace.
When I reach the goal I imagine the smile upon your
face.
Though I can no longer see that beautiful grin, the love
you had shines from me within.
The knowledge you bestowed upon your eldest daughter,
is being passed to your other children and some to their
father.
It's been almost a year but still feels like yesterday, I

can't stand to wake up and not see your darling face.
I miss you Mom, and can't wait to see you again.
You were more than just a mother, you were my best
friend.

10. Grief-share

When loving you meant forgetting me,
I took the darker path of the forging while being seized.
Led to some pretty wild places- I won't deny it.
Cut you off,
came back-
another cycle that's tiresome.
I grew weary,
lost myself,
lost my spark,
lost my shine.
You haunt me in ways that I cannot even hide.
Yet I gained something so precious, so invaluable, so
intensely mesmerizing.
A gift of God that I know came with the right timing.
If you feel like this is about you- it is.
Adult by the world's standards,
but inside was just a kid.

11. Sankalpa

Set the intention and be clear in your desires.
Seeing beyond the reality of the muck and the mire.
Internal dedication and a muscle to be exercised.
Yes, I am speaking of the mind.
And heart, how it aligns with your essence.
Speak life into others and watch as they transform in
your presence.
Firm will and mustered strength of the battles within.
Awareness that your sight will determine the win.
Eyes that see, yes, but I'm referencing the internal guide.
It's undenial once you've discovered the third-eye.
Kundalini awakened.
Spiral serpant unlocked.
Don't try to fight it, it cannot be blocked.
The experience takes over and you're thrown about.
Mentally ravished with an emotional drought.
Then light seeps in and it all makes sense.
The somatic memories of a world rooted in sin.
You'll overcome it, you see.
You have to- what is will be.
New levels achieved and an accomplishment, no doubt.
Meditate, my dear
Breathe in-
Breathe out.

12. WISDOM

Woman, tell me again;
Is this about you?
Supervised. trained to tackle, entrusted to
Discern.
One love,
Mama <3

13. Alphebetic tragedy

5.31-6.22-7.6.

Apple watches.

Braving.

Chosen by choice? Cough and sneeze count.

Daily yoga.

Enso.

Friends with complications.

Ghosting and going camping.

Happy days and hellacious nights.

Insight gained.

Juxtiposition obtained.

Kroger groceries.

Long heart to hearts.

Memories to last a lifetime.

Narcissism.

Oppression.

Perfection.

Quarls

Running away

Synergetic Systems.

Tantra.

Undeniably the best mistake

Values defined.

Walkie-talkies with a best friend.

Xanthic.

Yours, mine, and ours.

Zoo passes.

14. History of...

Emotional regulation, Distress tolerance, and coping skills.
A toolkit for when the battle is uphill.
Limited emotional vocabulary-
Bindings of the tongue and flesh.
Scars turned to open wounds- they're fresh.
Time has a funny way of uncovering what's hidden.
Lustful pride with an ego that was smitten.
Secrets and excuses while the stories were being written.
Expressive nature with a robust inner-life.
It was never unknown, your face showed the strife.
Denial and depression the cycles repeated.
Turns out the sunshine was all that was needed.
Solace in the solar flares and memories in the eclipses.
Let ears that hear soak up the hope of this script, sis.

15. SHALOM embodiment

I let the poetry flow,
It comes with the know-
how to speak into minds, hearts, and souls.
The words that I speak grow
with each syllable that you allow to sink deeper into the
psyche.
This might be
 the most profound rhyme I've written yet....
NEVER forget
The insight gained from adventures and exploration of
the great,
vast experiences that a life of misguided steps can take
you on.
HEAR my song.
The lyrics of my heartbeat pouring into you.
The you who is open
the you who is kind
the you who is- beating after beating-
still TRYING.
Trying to connect
Trying to be true
Accomplishing Authenticity and seeing it through.
Establishing boundaries,
 searching for peace.

Not letting go of the piece(s)
that create the exquisite artwork that
so wonderfully, intentionally
encompasses all that you strive to be.
Again, SHALOM means peace.

16. A Letter To My Past Self

The life within-
abundant and varying.
The emotions you feel..
you'll keep on carrying..
The hurt, the pain, the grief, and the joy.
The life you once knew, tossed out like a toy.
The life you once knew, lost over a boy.
You matured- you see- and the cost was great.
Those steps you're taking, some would call fate.
Serenity prayer echoing in my ear.
A coping skill that became a lifeline when all I knew was
fear.
Fear of the unknown and of stories untold.
Mourning losses of the mind, body, and soul.
Appearing so tender, so passive, so mild.
So naive, so selfless, so polite, and so wild.
Rebel heart, progressive mind, focused on losing time.
In others, in the community- out of sight, out of mind
Not true, you see, disappearing is not the cure.
Rash, life-changing decisions, made in an instance causes
quite the stir.
Choices made under duress,
leaves you emotionally naked with no shade and no rest.
Negative spirals, deep dives in a selfish way.

Grown enough to admit that I had my days.
Shrew, but what could I do?
Uncover the truth.
The truths of dark imaginings and a cold, twisted view.
Goodness it's so pleasant to be rid of you.

17. Ode to Future Me

A simple play on words.

The success, the earnings, the literacy desired.
Hard work, deep effort, achieved, acquired.
The words you speak
The company you keep.
The rooms where your presence is appre-ciated,
with a valued attitude.
Ambiance created, you set the mood.
Nothing easy comes to the quaint of spirit.
Words words words, you didn't want to hear it.
LOOK AT YOU NOW!
Such couthe, such grace.
On track and ahead, you set the pace.
Earned, with earnings multiplied ten-fold.
Another story begging to be told.
Accept it, embrace it, it's seen, it's felt.
Manifesting things unspoken and untold.
Millenial mindset.
My ode to being owed.

18. Mental Health Awareness

Concepts locked within the books of the elite.
The teachings of overcoming ineptness and defeat.
The practices they hold so encouraging and concrete.
Appearing so complex in the words that describe them.
Words like cognitive and dialectical meant to shy those
away whom desire it.
Take control of how you speak to yourself in watch what
transpires.
Become aware of those ANTs- those automatic negative
thoughts we all acquire.
Flip the flow and flip the switch.
Intentionality will allow you to become equipped...
With the tools of the privledged and the knowledge held
by the squires.
Mental health awareness.
I'm sharing the power.

19. Roots

Being brown in a pale world.
Appalachian trails and the Underground Railroad.
Walking the stores looking for the rarity of a reflection
of what I see.
Nope, not that one- it doesn't look like me.
Rural America and rebel flagged backroads.
A backwoods town tucked away in Southeastern Ohio.
Covert rules tell the stories of behavior for what I know.
I have a history of being a Muticultural Geneological
Center board member.
Native roots that run deep, just trying to remember.
The pride, the culture, the ways of my people.
Three-fifths compromise, to some we're not equal.
The Trail of Tears existing pains me to my core.
Never forget the bloodlines that pour into my sores.

20. Sanctity

There's a sanctity in knowing the depth of a having a home-base.
A place where you can reflect, relax, and relate.
The burden's lifted and connection is present.
Here on Earth, but it's a slice of heaven.
Having what is yours to call home.
No more abandonment, no more empty souls.
The perpetuity of the nights you thought would last forever.
Now mere memories in a world far away that you've surrendered.
A warm blanket, a robe, the AC set just right.
Snuggled up with those you love with electricity and a movie night.
Working utilities that are paid in full.
A liveable wage in a world where this is unknown.
Blessings on blessings, I don't take them lightly,
I'll sleep peacefully knowing those dark years are behind me.

21. "Hello"

It's guilt mixed with pleasure mixed with fear mixed
with pride.
Vulnerability so real, it's undeniable to hide.
"I went there"
"I did that"
I say shamelessly.
Welcome to your new understanding of the one who is
me.

www.ingramcontent.com/pod-product-compliance
Lightning Source LLC
LaVergne TN
LVHW010944200726

843509LV00013B/2287